DAVID BECKHAM
BORN TO PLAY

By B. A. Roth
with photographs

Grosset & Dunlap • New York

The Date: June 7, 2002

The Place: the Sapporo Dome, Sapporo, Japan

The Event: the 2002 World Cup: England vs. Argentina

David Beckham lined up in the tunnel with his team. He heard his English teammates shouting. They were getting psyched up to face Argentina in their second match in the 2002 World Cup. Their first game, against Sweden, had ended in a tie. They knew they must win this match to stay in the tournament.

The soccer teams from England and Argentina were big rivals. The last time the two teams had met was at the 1998 World Cup. During that game, Beckham fouled Argentina's team captain. As a result, he received a "red card" penalty. When a player gets a red card, he must

leave the game. Without Beckham playing, England was down one player. Argentina won that game by a score of 4–3. Newspaper reporters blamed Beckham for the loss. They said that if Beckham had finished the game, England might have won. Now, four years later, Beckham had a chance to redeem himself.

As Beckham raced onto the field, the England fans cheered. His heart was pounding. The battle was about to begin. But Beckham had a problem: He had broken a bone in his left foot two months earlier. He wasn't sure how well he'd be able to play.

It took a while for him to warm up, but Beckham finally had the ball. He was near the net. Should he shoot or pass? Suddenly, an Argentine player knocked him over. Beckham was sure it was a foul. He was positive that his team would get a free kick. But the referee did not see it that way.

Now another English player, Michael Owen, had the ball. As he ran, he was tripped by an Argentine player. This was a foul for sure.

A penalty shot was given. Beckham was going to take the shot. Beckham was a great penalty shooter. He put the ball down and got ready. Beckham stared at

the net. He looked at the ball. Then he ran.
It felt as though everything around him
were spinning. Beckham took a deep breath
and kicked the ball as hard as he could.

GOAL!

Flashbulbs popped. The crowd roared.
Beckham's teammates pounced on him.

But one question ran through Beckham's
mind: Was his goal enough to win the
game?

The second half
began. Each team
played hard. England
held off Argentina.
Beckham's team
had won! The
disappointment of
losing the previous
World Cup game was
eased.

Young Beckham

On May 2, 1975, in the East End of
London, England, a Manchester United
fan was born. The baby's parents, David
Edward Alan Beckham and Sandra
Georgina West, were huge fans of the
soccer team. Of course, they would raise
their son to be a fan, too.

David's Mom and Dad, proud parents of a soccer star!

There were plenty of London teams that the Beckhams could support: Chelsea, Arsenal, and Tottenham, to name a few. But the family picked Man U. For each game, the family—including sisters Joanne and Lynne—would travel more than three hours north to watch home matches at Old Trafford, the team's stadium.

Growing up, David was a quiet kid. He didn't focus much on his school studies, but he loved art class. And, of course, he loved sports: basketball, baseball, rugby, and soccer. He was especially crazy about soccer (or football, as it is called outside the U.S.).

David played for different local teams in his hometown of Chingford. He played for his elementary school, Chase Lane Primary. And when he was older, he was a member of Chingford High's team.

But back then he was best known for joining the Ridgeway Rovers when he was seven years old. The team played in a youth league called "the Sunday League." The group was for boys ages seven to eleven. David liked the group. And he was a great player. During his three years with the Rovers, David scored more than one hundred goals!

One of the Rovers' coaches was David's dad. David was smaller than the other boys on his team. "I used to get my share of knocks," David recalls. But his dad developed special strategies for him. When they practiced at Larkswood Park, his dad always said that the best thing to do when you're knocked down is to get right up!

The Rovers played matches all across Europe, like in Germany and Holland.

David played with the team until he was eleven.

After that, he enrolled in the Bobby Charlton Soccer School. Bobby Charlton, a famous Manchester United player (1954–1973), started and ran the clinic for talented young players. David competed and won first place in Charlton's National Skills Final. In that tournament, David was judged on his dribbling, passing, and other soccer skills. His prize was a week's visit to train with Futbol Club Barcelona in Spain. David was excited. He knew that this trip would be a chance to meet some of Spain's and England's great coaches.

It was clear to David's parents and coaches that he had natural ability. But David also worked hard. Very hard. He was always trying to improve his skills. David knew that one day he would become a professional soccer player. But which team would he play for? His dream was to become a Manchester United player.

England's top soccer teams always had scouts looking out for young players. Man U had scouted David. But they didn't ask him to play for them yet.

In 1988, David started training with the youth division of the Tottenham Hotspurs' "school of excellence." The Spurs were a powerful London soccer team. They had won many championships. The Spurs offered him a contract. But David turned it down. He was waiting for Man U.

On David's thirteenth birthday, Manchester's legendary manager Alex Ferguson met with him during a Manchester home game. Ferguson had heard a lot about David. He thought

David could do great things for the team.

Ferguson gave David what he had been waiting for: a youth training contract! David would start as a trainee and then, when he was ready, he would move up to the professional squad, also known as "the First Team." For Beckham, this was a dream come true!

Hard years of practice and training followed. But by the age of sixteen, David, along with the help of teammates Nicky Butt, Paul Scholes, Ryan Giggs, and Gary Neville—"the Famous Five"—helped his team win the 1992 Football Association Youth Cup.

David quickly moved up to the First Team level. And on January 22, 1993, he signed a professional contract with Manchester.

On April 2, 1995, David Beckham

made his league debut with Manchester
United's First Team in a game against
Leeds. He took over the position of Andrei
Kanchelskis, a Russian midfielder who had
been traded.

Manchester United had a long history of
superstars: Bobby Charlton, George Best,
Dennis Law, and Eric Cantona. Beckham
knew he had to prove himself. He was
a good player who played with focus,
determination, and control. But Beckham

had one very special quality: a fantastic kick. With his powerful right leg, he was able to make great crosses and long shots.

One of his most famous kicks was a shot taken from the halfway line during a game against Wimbledon on August 17, 1996. In this game, Beckham spotted the opposing team's goalie, Neil Sullivan, standing just outside the goal line. With all the power he had, David chipped the ball with a spin. The ball flew over Sullivan's head and behind him into the net. It was an unbelievable shot! David's teammates were amazed—and so was David! The fans roared. The announcer covering the game said: "David Beckham—surely an England player of the future!"

The Best Years Ever?

David Beckham was gaining lots of fans. On the field, people admired his fantastic kick and his cool playing style. Off the field, they admired his good looks. In fact, some people called him England's most eligible bachelor. He was making good money now and driving fancy cars. What more could he want?

In 1996, David met someone he would later call "the girl of my dreams." The girl was Victoria Adams. The rest of the world knew her as Posh Spice, of the pop singing group the Spice Girls.

David and Victoria had a lot in common, which is why Simon Fuller, the Spice Girls' manager (and originator of *American Idol*), thought the two would hit it off. Victoria is from Goff's Oak, which is only a fifteen-minute ride from David's hometown. Both were very driven and committed to their work. Both had dreams of raising a family.

Fuller introduced David to Victoria. They liked each other right away. At first, David and Victoria tried to keep their relationship a secret. They didn't want to be followed around by reporters. Eventually, word got out about "Posh and Becks." Their photos were in newspapers and magazines.

On the soccer field, things were going well, too. Manchester United had a great 1996–1997 season. They won the Football Association League (FA League) Championship. The FA League is made up of all the soccer teams in England.

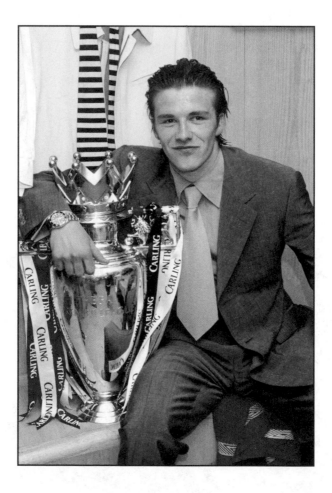

Manchester also won the Premier League title. The Premier League is made up of the top teams from England.

Also in 1997, David was voted the Professional Footballers Association Young Player of the Year. Then David got an even bigger honor. He was asked to join England's soccer team. David would still play for Man U, but as a member of England's team he would face teams from other countries. He might also get the chance to compete in the World Cup. The World Cup is a soccer tournament that is played every four years. Teams from all over the world can play in the World Cup.

The 1997–1998 season wasn't so great for Manchester United. They lost the Premier League championship to Arsenal. But 1998 was a World Cup year, and England was in. England's first game, against Tunisia, ended with a win. They lost their second game, against Romania. But in the game against Colombia, Beckham scored the winning goal.

England's rival, Argentina, was next. Soon after the second half started, the Argentine captain, Diego Simeone, knocked Beckham from behind. From the ground, Beckham responded by kicking Simeone back. The referee gave David a "red card"—Beckham was out of the game. England was short a player. The game ended with the teams tied at 2–2.

Then the game went into a penalty shootout. Argentina won 4–3. The press blamed the loss on Beckham. Newspapers ran front-page headlines like: "What an Idiot." When David returned to England, he found that he was no longer loved by his fans. In fact, most English fans hated him. David was angry. He felt he had let his fans down. But he told himself, "It's a round world. Whenever you're down, you build yourself back up."

After the World Cup loss in 1998, fans were not happy with David. And David was not happy with his fans. David had always been a quiet person. But now he was getting angry back at his fans. He began shouting at them. He acted rudely in public. Negative reports were written about him in newspapers and magazines. He was staying out late. He was speeding in his car.

The 1998–1999 season arrived. David Beckham decided it was time to change his image. He did not like all the negative publicity. He decided to work harder during practices. He had his head in the game.

Beckham's plan to bring things around again worked—both on the field and off. In 1999, David Beckham and Victoria Adams got married. The fairy-tale wedding took place at an Irish castle outside Dublin on July 4, 1999. Many stars attended the wedding. It was reported to have cost five hundred thousand pounds!

On the field, Manchester United was having a great year. They became the only team in history to win the Treble. (A Treble is awarded when a team wins three championships.) They won the Premiership Cup, the European Cup, and the FA Cup. David was voted Best Midfielder and Most Valuable Player.

David's status as a soccer superstar was at an all-time high. His salary at Man U was one of the highest in the league: seventy-five thousand pounds per week! Later, he would demand and receive almost two hundred thousand pounds per week—the highest ever in Manchester's history. On top of his salary, Beckham's movie-star looks earned him endorsements. He appeared in Adidas,

Vodafone, and Pepsi commercials.

In August of 1999, David and Victoria bought a seven-bedroom mansion on twenty-four acres in Sawbridgeworth, which is outside of London. Reporters called their multi-million-dollar home "Beckingham Place."

Alex Ferguson, Man U's manager, didn't like all the attention David and his

family were getting. To Ferguson, David's family time meant time away from the team. When the team traveled and stayed together in a hotel, the Beckhams would often stay together at another hotel. When team members organized activities like playing golf, David would vacation instead with his family.

David did not like to hang out with his fellow soccer players. He often went home right after games. Ferguson felt that David wasn't trying hard enough. Were David's days playing for his dream team coming to an end?

He's Got Style!

David Beckham
brought more than
good soccer to his
fans—he brought a
sense of style. Off
the field, he wore
fashionable clothes
and drove expensive
cars. He had a
handsome face and
an athletic body—
and tattoos.

The first tattoo
David got was
located on his lower
back and it says "Brooklyn," in honor of
his first son. David later had the names of
his two other sons—Cruz and Romeo—

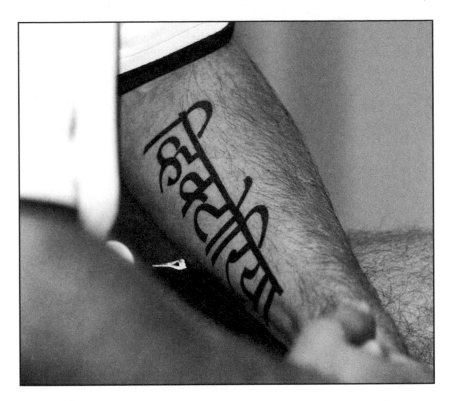

added to his back. On his left arm is
Victoria's name written in Hindi (and
rumored to have been spelled wrong).
On his right arm is "VII," the Roman
numeral seven, Beckham's team number.
Louis Malloy, a Manchester, England,
tattoo artist, has created all of Beckham's
skin work.

Beckham has had a lot of different

hairstyles over the years, too: the bleach-blond rag top, dark hair with light streaks, a Mohawk, and a shaved head. The styles were not only entertaining, they created a following. Beckham's fans were turning up at Old Trafford with shaved heads. And in Japan, women wore their hair in colorful Mohawk cuts.

Whether he was on or off the field, David Beckham certainly knew how to make a statement!

Adiós, England

David's next season with Manchester, 2000–2001, started off well. He scored an amazing sixteen goals. But then he started to slow down. He looked tired. What was happening to this soccer superstar?

Alex Ferguson was not happy with Beckham. It soon became clear that he wanted David off the team. Ferguson thought that Beckham had changed.

When David first joined the team, he was quiet. He worked hard. He played with determination. Now, David was a superstar. Sure, he still played well, but Ferguson did not like David's attitude. And he did not like Victoria. Ferguson told Sports Illustrated: ". . . his life changed when [David] met his wife. She's in pop and David got another image. He's developed this 'fashion thing.' I saw his transition into a different person."

Ferguson knew it would be hard to fire Beckham. So he decided to force him to leave the team. Ferguson did not start David in many games. Sometimes he was used as a substitute. Sometimes he was not played at all. Ferguson also criticized David a lot. And, if the team lost, he often blamed the loss on David.

But David was working hard playing

for England. On November 15, 2000, he was promoted to team captain. The team was hoping to qualify for the 2002 World Cup. If they were able to either beat or tie Greece, they'd be in.

The game began. England was down by a score of 2–1. The team was not playing well. But Beckham turned things around. He nailed a penalty kick. England tied the game. They had made it to the World Cup!

Then disaster struck. During a Man U match against Deportivo in Spain, an opponent slid into David with a two-foot tackle, shattering a bone in David's foot. David was devastated. With the World Cup coming up, all of England worried if he'd recover in time. Even the Prime Minister and the Queen of England asked for the country's prayers.

Miraculously, Beckham's foot healed in time. England played well and reached the quarterfinals. But, in the end, they were no match for the Brazilians. A powerful kick by Brazil's Ronaldinho

completely caught England by surprise
and ended it 2–1. Although Beckham
was upset at the loss, he showed great
leadership by comforting the goalie,
David Seaman, who had let the shot in.

Back with Man U, things were not

going well. One day, after a loss to
Arsenal for the FA Cup, Ferguson yelled
at David in the locker room. In front of
the team, Ferguson blamed Beckham for
the loss. David yelled back at Ferguson.
David's teammates were shocked. Players
never dared talk back to their coaches!
In frustration, Ferguson kicked a soccer
shoe in David's direction. The shoe hit
David just above the eye, leaving a big
cut. Later, Ferguson apologized. But he
never admitted whether he hit David on
purpose or not.

David did not know
what to do. He did
not want to play for a
manager who did not
want him. But could
he leave his dream
team?

Then, something strange happened. After a loss to Real Madrid, Spain's top soccer club, one of the players came up to David during the game. "Are you coming to play for us?" Other Real players looked at David and smiled as if they knew something.

Real's President, Florentino Pérez, had recruited some of the world's best players: Luis Figo, of Portugal; Zinedine Zidane, the Algerian-born Frenchman; and Ronaldo, of Brazil. And now they wanted David Beckham. David

started to talk secretly with the managers of Real Madrid.

Now David had to make the decision of his life. His best advice came from Victoria: "This is a huge change in our lives: a different country, a different way of life. You play your soccer—and you'd better play well—and I'll do my music. And for the rest of it, we'll be where you need to be: you, me, and the boys. The family." With that kind of support, David called his agent, Tony Stephens, and simply said: "Real Madrid."

On July 1, 2003, after thirteen years of playing for Manchester United, David Beckham officially signed a four-year contract with Real Madrid.

Hola, España

In June of 2003, the Beckhams
flew to Japan. It was part of a tour on
which David would have interviews and
promote his sponsors in Japan, Vietnam,
Malaysia, and Thailand. In total, his
commercial sponsors were paying him
approximately five million dollars—that's
more than he was paid in one year to

play soccer—to promote their products.
Japanese fans were wild about Beckham.
They turned out at the airports to greet
him. Victoria was also a big draw for
women who loved her music.

Real Madrid was hoping Beckham

would generate a similar response in soccer-mad Spain. *Marca*, the Spanish sports magazine, declared him "King Midas of football."

David started off the season right for Real Madrid. His first match was against FC Tokyo in Japan. Beckham scored with one of his famous free kicks. Real Madrid beat the Japanese team 3–0. And

in his first match at Real Madrid's home
stadium, Santiago Bernabéu, he assisted
Roberto Carlos in a goal. The Real
Madrid fans went wild as their team beat
Marseille 4–2.

David was glad to play for Real Madrid.
But he also really wanted to fit in with

his teammates. "What really interested me," he said, "was the atmosphere among the players, the way they get along . . . I'm not coming here to be the main star, I'm coming here to enjoy playing with these great players and being in this great city." Although Real Madrid had a losing season that year, Beckham scored five goals in his fifteen matches.

While he was showing his talents on the field, off the field the Spanish fans were going crazy for him. Mobs of reporters shadowed Beckham at every restaurant, shop, and social event he attended. The fans followed, calling out, *"Guapo, guapo!"* ("Handsome, handsome!")

Fans flocked to the stadium to see Beckham play. The year before Beckham started playing for Real Madrid, fans bought nine hundred thousand soccer shirts. Once Beckham started playing, over three million were sold!

But the first year in Spain was hard for Beckham. Victoria and the boys did not move to Madrid. Victoria said that her children were not ready to move. Some people thought that her work on a solo record was what was keeping her in London. Others thought that Beckham planned to return to England after a year. David had three years left on his contract with Real Madrid, but there were rumors that he might return to London in an Arsenal or Chelsea jersey. Beckham, however, remained committed to his new team. "I've been here for one season and it feels like the job's not done yet," David said.

Victoria and the kids moved to Madrid in time for the second season. David was

happy. He played well on the team. But
Real only reached the quarterfinals of the
Championship League.

The next year, 2006, was a World Cup
year. Even though Beckham was living in
Spain, he still played for England. And
England was in the World Cup. Beckham
played well. His free kicks, crosses, and
goals helped England win their early
games. In their opening match of the
final round, England defeated Ecuador in

a sixtieth-minute free kick by Beckham. But the victory was short. David hurt his leg in the next game against Portugal. He left the match in the fifty-second minute. The team lost 3–1 in a penalty shootout.

England was out of the World Cup.

After the game, David held a press conference. He announced that he was stepping down as team captain. "I have lived the dream," he said with tears in his

eyes. "I am extremely proud to have worn the armband and been captain of England, and for that I will always be grateful."

David still wanted to play for England. But the team got a new coach, Steve McClaren. McClaren soon announced that David would not return as a player.

David returned

to Spain for the 2006–2007 season, but things there were not much better. There was a new president and coach of Real Madrid. Coach Fabio Capello turned out not to be a fan of David's. He mainly used David as a sub.

On January 10, 2007, Real's sporting director announced that they would not renew Beckham's contract.

The next day, the Los Angeles Galaxy, part of the American Major League Soccer (MLS), announced that a $250 million, five-year agreement had been reached with David Beckham to play for their team. *Adiós*, España, *hola*, America.

California,
Here We Come

MLS soccer fans were thrilled at the news of David coming to America. In the United States, soccer is not as popular as baseball, basketball, or football. But with Beckham coming to play for the MLS, maybe more people would watch the sport.

Then the world of soccer got more amazing news. After being dropped from the England team, Beckham was asked back. In his first appearance with the team, in a match against Brazil on June 1, 2007, Beckham crossed to John Terry for a goal.

And there was more—even though Beckham's contract with Real Madrid wasn't renewed, he played with the team in the Spanish league champsionship game against Mallorca on June 12, 2007. Beckham's amazing cross to Ronaldo helped set up a goal in Madrid's ultimate 3–1 win. The cheers for Beckham could be heard practically around the world!

* * *

David Beckham lined up in the tunnel with his teammates. He was waiting for the Galaxy game to begin. He could hear the American fans shouting.

David ran onto the field. His heart was racing. He looked at the crowd. David felt happy and proud. He was happy that he was doing what he loved. And he was proud that all these American fans were watching the great game of soccer.